ROBLOX
MEGA HITS

100% UNOFFICIAL

First published in Great Britain 2022 by 100% Unofficial,
part of Farshore

An imprint of HarperCollins*Publishers*
1 London Bridge Street, London SE1 9GF
www.farshore.co.uk

HarperCollinsPublishers
1st Floor, Watermarque Building, Ringsend Road
Dublin 4, Ireland

Written by Kevin Pettman

This book is an original creation by Farshore
© 2022 HarperCollins*Publishers*

ISBN 978 0 7555 0263 9
Printed in Italy
1

ONLINE SAFETY FOR YOUNGER FANS

Spending time online is great fun! Here are a few simple rules to help younger fans stay safe and
keep the internet a great place to spend time:
- Never give out your real name – don't use it as your username.
- Never give out any of your personal details.
- Never tell anybody which school you go to or how old you are.
- Never tell anybody your password except a parent or a guardian.
- Be aware that you must be 13 or over to create an account on many sites.
Always check the site policy and ask a parent or guardian for permission before registering.
- Always tell a parent or guardian if something is worrying you.
Stay safe online. Any website addresses listed in this book are correct at the time of going to print.
However, Farshore is not responsible for content hosted by third parties. Please be aware that online
content can be subject to change and websites can contain content that is unsuitable for children.
We advise that all children are supervised when using the internet.

Stay safe online. Farshore is not responsible for content hosted by third parties.

MIX
Paper from
responsible sources
FSC™ C007454

ROBLOX
MEGA HITS

CONTENTS

GAME ON!

If you're a fan of action-packed games, then Roblox is the perfect place for you! Millions of players around the world join in the fun and enjoy taking on challenges and battling to be the best. Roblox games offer it all, from slick player-versus-player adventures to exciting quests, creations, role-playing, survival tests and much more. Team up with friends or go solo – only you will decide your destiny!

These pages are stuffed with super stats and strategies. You'll explore some of the top titles and what it takes to master them, discovering tips and tricks to take your gaming to the next level.

It's time to load up and start the action!

JAILBREAK

Cops versus criminals ... that's what Jailbreak is all about! It's a simple idea but with so many possibilities that'll keep you hooked. Whether you choose to be good or bad, Jailbreak delivers every time you jump in and mixes the best bits of the role-playing, adventure and shooter genres.

CREATED BY: BADIMO
YEAR: 2017
GENRE: TOWN & CITY

TOP TIP

As a prisoner, you can punch the power box to open the jail fence, but this is noisy and attracts the officers!

Escape Plan

Choose to be a prisoner or the police. As part of the criminal gang, your first task is getting past the perimeter. Stealing a keycard, blowing up walls, hitting power boxes and slinking through the slimy sewers are all valid paths to freedom.

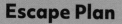

Avoid Arrest

Outside the prison walls, it's classic cops versus robbers action. Use vehicles to speed around the city, then raid the gun store for weapons to add to your inventory. You'll need firepower to execute your heists without a hitch!

Season Updates

Regular updates and fresh seasonal content keep fans coming back for more. Developer duo Badimo were inspired by the Redwood Prison and Prison Life games, which led to this huge hit that has scooped up billions of plays and plenty of BLOXY awards!

Double Trouble

Become familiar with the best places to rob. The museum needs two criminals, one to blow a hole in the roof and another to drop in and scoop the loot. Plot your escape, avoiding the trigger alarms on your exit before you dash to the criminal base to cash in on your rapid raid.

Crime Spree

Breaking into the jewellery store and the bank should also be on your to-do list. The easiest way to enter is with a keycard, but dynamite is also effective! Head to the vaults, avoiding the red laser alarms, and then load up on the stash of cash.

Switch Sides

If you want to play the good guy, select the police officer role at the start or click the switch team icon to begin enforcing the law instead of breaking it! You can even go plain-clothes to spring surprise justice on unsuspecting criminals.

Map It Out

As an officer, learn the habits of the bad guys. Try camping out on the roof of the jewellery store, ready for when robbers burst out, or wait for them to pop up from the prison sewer. Keep an eye on the bank, gas stations and the train as these are hotspots for criminal activity.

Sky High

Switching to the skies is a clever tactic on either side of the law. While helicopters can be shot down, they are difficult to target and can get to locations much quicker than cars. The helicopter is also free and spawns at the police HQs and the military base.

Daily Contract

Contracts are refreshed daily and reward you with XP if you complete them. Some common contracts are to arrest someone with a certain bounty level or pop a player's wheels with a gun. Some are harder than others, but don't give up!

TOP TIP

Stop others from racing away in your vehicle by keeping it locked. The lock button is on the bottom right of the screen, turning blue when your machine is secure!

Ocean Scene

Don't just think that all the action is on the land. Cross the ocean by helicopter to reach a special heist on the huge cargo ship. Use the rope to pick up a container, then drop it at a warehouse for cash rewards. The police can also pocket money from the ship by dumping a container in the water.

ARSENAL

The aim of Arsenal is to shoot accurately and eliminate other players – as simple as that! The gameplay is frantic, but as your experience develops, you'll learn how to boss the rounds and come out on top. After Arsenal's revamp in 2018, millions flocked to the game to make it one of the most popular shooters on Roblox. Time to get locked and loaded, folks!

CREATED BY: ROLVE COMMUNITY
YEAR: 2015
GENRE: FIRST-PERSON SHOOTER

TOP TIP

In Arsenal, players run quicker when holding a melee weapon compared to having a firearm out.

Standard Stuff

There are several modes to try out, from the standard game to gun rotation and railgun royale. In standard, the task is to be the first team or player to reach 33 eliminations. After each takedown, your weapon will change, meaning you need to be a master of all skills to be crowned champion.

Golden Glory

After kill 32, your weapon will become the golden knife. One more elimination with this tool will bag you the victory! Striking with a melee weapon is very tricky, so you'll need to sneak up and then strike. Keep an eye on your health and try to top it up with healing items collected from your defeated enemies.

Raise Your Game

Secure the high spots on a map to gain an advantage. Standing on top of buildings and walls means you can stay hidden and snipe from a safe distance. The element of surprise is vital as you try to turn up the heat on the enemy!

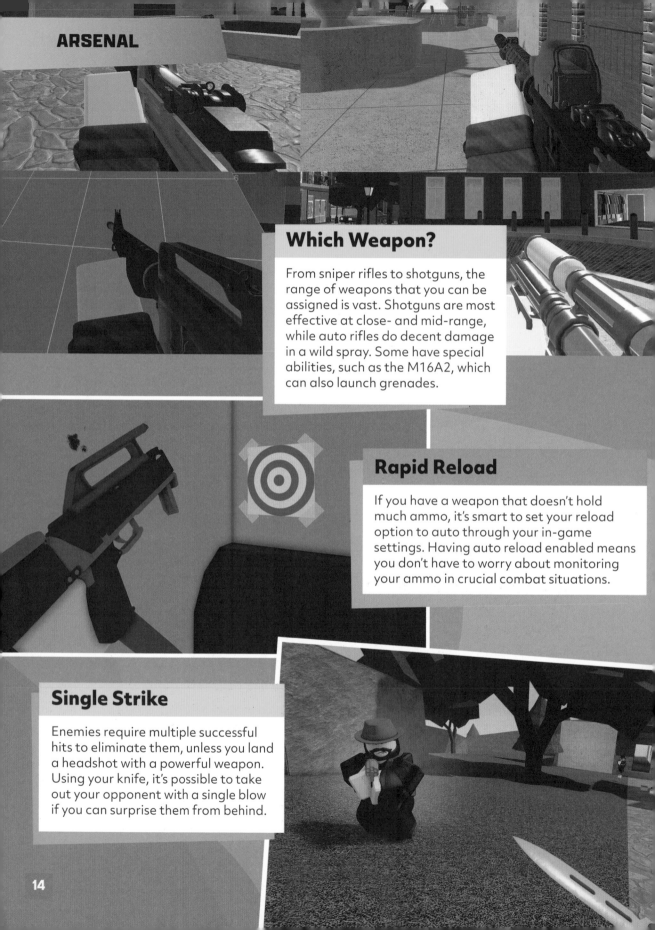

ARSENAL

Which Weapon?

From sniper rifles to shotguns, the range of weapons that you can be assigned is vast. Shotguns are most effective at close- and mid-range, while auto rifles do decent damage in a wild spray. Some have special abilities, such as the M16A2, which can also launch grenades.

Rapid Reload

If you have a weapon that doesn't hold much ammo, it's smart to set your reload option to auto through your in-game settings. Having auto reload enabled means you don't have to worry about monitoring your ammo in crucial combat situations.

Single Strike

Enemies require multiple successful hits to eliminate them, unless you land a headshot with a powerful weapon. Using your knife, it's possible to take out your opponent with a single blow if you can surprise them from behind.

Extra Assistance

Don't think that you only get the glory by landing the killing blow against an opponent. If you record a hit but someone else on your team completes the kill, you'll still be rewarded with a weapon upgrade. This is called an assist.

FUN FACT

ROLVe Community also makes the cool Counter Blox game. These creators are totally ruling the FPS scene!

Custom Options

Away from the pressure of surviving in a shootout, Arsenal also offers lots of customisable extras. There are character and weapon skins, emotes, effects and bundles to switch up your on-screen look.

Lift Off

Here's a cool way to get a height advantage over your opposition. If you have the rocket launcher, RPG or twin-powered DBS firearm, just hit the jump button and shoot at the ground. You will be launched into the air and get a bird's eye view of the enemies around you.

DUNGEON QUEST

The all-action adventures of Dungeon Quest willl unleash the fantasy fighter in you by dropping you in a world of powerful weapons, arcane spells and endless battles! Create a character to begin your quest through dozens of dungeons and fend off hundreds of scary foes along the way.

CREATED BY: **VCAFFY**

YEAR: **2018**

GENRE: **ADVENTURE / ROLE PLAYING**

FUN FACT

If you have Robux, make yourself stand out with the VIP pass. You'll get a VIP chat tag, rainbow text chat and exclusive king and queen characters!

Wave After Wave

Playing solo or in a team, your quest is to run through dangerous dungeons and defeat waves of terrifying mobs with a variety of magical weapons. Once they are wiped out, the dungeon door opens to the final room where the big boss comes to life!

Boss Battle

The bosses usually have much greater health than regular enemies, so be prepared for a long scrap. Use your weapons to hack and slash at the boss's health bar, and dodge away to avoid taking damage. The reward for victory can be anything from new armour or weapons to a powerful spell.

Dungeon Decision

There are more than ten dungeons to visit, including a desert temple, pirate island and samurai palace. You'll need to raise your level to access the tougher dungeons, so start finishing rooms to boost your experience! Dungeon Quest has five difficulty settings too, ranging from easy to nightmare.

Hard Going

You can opt into the hardcore mode when you start a game. This means you'll only have one life, but as a reward for your bravery, you'll pick up twice the loot! But if you are defeated, you'll lose everything and have to start all over again.

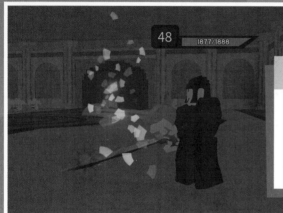

Pure Class

Get used to the different classes of fighters in this game. As a warrior, you'll focus on physical power and the damage you can deal with a sword in hand. When levelling up, skill points can be used to boost your stamina and physical levels.

Magic Mage

The mage is the other main damage-dealing class. They use magical powers to inflict damage at a distance and stay out of the clutches of monsters. They are focused on the spell power of their equipment, with very little afforded to their physical power.

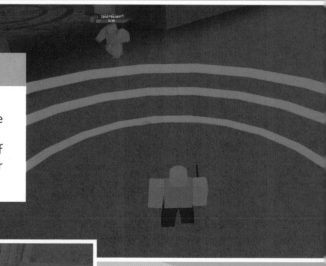

Tanks Very Much

The tank role helps to protect players in a team. A tank uses powerful armour and unleashes mainly ranged attacks, but their primary purpose is to taunt waves of mobs and keep the attention away from teammates. The Taunt function can't be used In a boss battle though.

Restore

Healers work to keep a team alive in a battle, something that becomes increasingly important in more difficult dungeons. The healer can produce spells to cast a healing circle that not only boosts them but also their teammates within the circle.

Attack Options

Weapons come in five rarities – common, uncommon, rare, epic and legendary. Whether it's a wand, sword, dagger or axe, each weapon has different strengths. You may find new ones while you're adventuring through dungeons too.

Defend

If you want to improve your skills, choose the wave defence option, which is on the left of the main skills and gear display screen. In this mode, hordes of mobs spawn at random gates, with enemy power levels increasing the further you progress!

Trade Time

Make trades to get your hands on powerful items others have found. Start by offering something from your inventory and your partner will do the same, at which point you can confirm the trade. Just beware that some items have level requirements, so you might not be able to use your new gear straight away.

19

ISLANDS

If you like farming, building, combat, adventure, trading and much more, then Islands is the perfect place for you! You start by extending your small island in the sky to bank coins, level up and receive XP. You can then use these assets to collect more items and make use of the Hub area, or venture to mob islands to fight daunting monsters.

CREATED BY: **EASY.GG**
YEAR: **2020**
GENRE: **ADVENTURE / SURVIVAL**

FUN FACT

The most in-game coins a player can have is 1.5 billion. That's a crazy stash of cash!

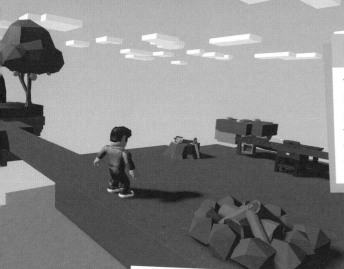

Basic Beginnings

Your island is small and basic, but you have enough at your fingertips to progress … if you know the right moves to make! Don't worry about falling off as you'll just reappear at the spawn point on your island.

First Moves

Begin by selecting your wooden axe and harvesting trees. Use the wood to craft a wooden pickaxe on your workbench and use the pickaxe to collect grass blocks. You can make a bridge with these blocks across to the next island. Ideally you want to reach the purple Hub portal sooner rather than later.

Get Growing

You can also make a plow, which will make the land suitable to plant seeds that will grow into crops. Look for berries, which replenish 20 health points and extras that can be sold at the Hub. Your farming XP rises with activities like this.

ISLANDS

Benchmark

When you harvest trees, saplings will appear in your inventory. Planting saplings will produce another tree in a few minutes. Upgrade your workbench to a basic workbench using harvested wood and iron ore. The crafting grid will tell you which resources you need to craft items now.

The Hub

Upon entering the Hub, you can stock up on iron ore, stone and coal by harvesting the many rocks there – have your pickaxe ready! The Hub is the central zone in Islands where trading can take place. Blocks, seeds and crops are valuable resources to buy or sell.

Village People

If you have enough coins, you can make a trade in the Hub with a merchant. There are usually around 12 of these characters, with others appearing in special events. They include Tom, who trades crops, Cletus (seeds), John (blocks) and Thomas (fish).

Fishy Story

Try a spot of fishing when you're inside the Hub or on the Desert or Slime Island. Fish can then be sold to Thomas or, if you catch salmon and carp, be composted together to craft basic fertilizer to help grow crops. Ten wood is needed to craft a wooden fishing rod. An iron rod, which catches more valuable species of swordfish and eel, needs 50 maple wood and 40 iron at level 20.

TOP TIP

The regen potion, which is crafted using starfruit, red mushroom and a potion bottle, restores 50 HP.

Visitors

Back on your island, keep an eye open for a merchant making a surprise visit to offer you a special trade. If you're not happy with these guys showing up, just hit the option that asks them to leave the island. Trades may be based on the season you're in, which changes every 24 hours.

Slime Time

Craft a simple wooden sword from 20 wood and venture to Slime Island from the Hub. All the mob islands are reached in sequence through portals, but you need the correct combat level in order to reach higher islands, such as Wizard Island and Diamond Mines.

Awesome Extras

Animals can also be cared for, bred or sold for coins. As you progress and become experienced, you'll have enough money for totems, which are items that spawn resources on your island, and to set up a campfire to smelt iron ore to make a powerful iron sword.

ROCITIZENS

RoCitizens has a long history in Roblox, offering slick city adventures that aren't all about saving the world. It has an impressive depth of tasks, jobs and minigames for players to enjoy. Set your avatar loose and start working, driving, creating a home and so much more!

CREATED BY: **FIREBRAND1**
YEAR: **2013**
GENRE: **TOWN AND CITY / ROLE-PLAYING**

TOP TIP

Buy special limited items from the shop and then trade them later for a higher price when they are off sale.

KER-CHING!

Super Sim

RoCitizens is a single-player RPG-style suburban simulator, where you can hang out with friends and explore the community. New players will meet helpful NPCs, such as Henry in the spawn area and Spencer in the car dealership, who will give you hints to explore new options.

Smartphone

You can tread your own path around RoCity. Feel free to wander around and see what the city has to offer you. You'll want to check your smartphone, as it controls things like your chats, parties, house and car set-up. Whether you're on foot or driving, the map tool is also very helpful in showing interesting locations.

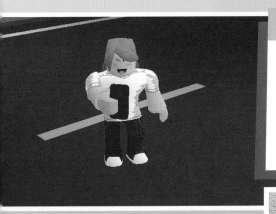

Job Hunt

RoCitizens has several job choices that offer a regular salary and bonuses, so you can buy more items and customise your world. You can be anything from a bus driver or cook to a police officer or nurse.

House Hunting

With cash building up from your job, it's time to set up your house and begin making a lovely home for yourself! Pick your blueprint from a wide variety, then select items to furnish it and create a look you love.

ISLAND ROYALE

Battle Royale-style games have exploded in recent years! Offering everything from manic shootouts and tactical team play, to build battles and character customisation, Island Royale is one of the very best. Your aim is to take out the other islanders to be the last player or team standing.

CREATED BY: **LORDJURRD**
YEAR: **2018**
GENRE: **BATTLE ROYALE / FIRST-PERSON SHOOTER**

FUN FACT

Match modes include solos, duos, squads, FFA (free for all), box fight and special limited time modes.

Early Game

You'll drop from a flying bus onto the map, choosing to land in one of the varied locations. Look for loot chests in buildings as you need a weapon straight away to defend yourself. Hopefully you'll scoop something powerful like a submachine gun.

Mats Matter

Build up your material levels by harvesting trees, buildings and cars, which will give you a stack of resources to build basic ramps and shelters for when you come under attack. Materials, weapons and items can also be picked up from eliminated players.

Which Weapons?

Weapons come in different rarities, starting at grey commons and rising to yellow mythics. The damage and fire rate will vary, with rifles great at mid and long range and machine guns being effective when the target is closer. Try them all out to see what you like the best.

4 - 18

In Order

Arrange your inventory so weapons and healing items are easy to access. Keep an eye on your health and shield bar at the bottom of the screen, and take cover while you consume a health kit or potion. The storm clock counts down too, reducing the area where you can hide and avoid damage.

LOOMIAN LEGACY

Inspired by epic monster-collection RPGs, Loomian Legacy is a globetrotting adventure where you collect various battle-ready critters, power them up and challenge the toughest trainers in the world to become the greatest Loomian Master ever to walk the land.

CREATED BY: LLAMA TRAIN STUDIO
YEAR: 2015
GENRE: TACTICAL RPG

TOP TIP

Loomians have different types, like water and fire, which each have their own strengths and weaknesses against certain types. Use a mix of types to gain an advantage.

Fight

Run

The Quest Begins

You'll start your adventure in Mitis Town, the home of the hero of Loomian Legacy: you! Your dad is studying a strange tablet at a nearby dig site, but when you visit the new discovery, the tablet breaks into shards that fly off around the land of Roria.

Battle Buddies

At the Loomian Laboratory, your father charges you with locating the fragments that have scattered across the land. But you won't be alone, you get to choose one of the laboratory's cute monster friends – a Loomian. Now you're a Loomian trainer!

Catching Fever

Once you have your Loomian sidekick, you can explore Roria and encounter more wild Loomians, which you can befriend using capture discs. There are over 200 creatures for you to find, battle and capture, and more are being added all the time!

Kabunga   LV5

Tactical Battle

Each Loomian has a unique move set that uses up the creature's energy points. Once the Loomian's energy is depleted, you must rest it to recover energy, but that could leave it open to attack! Energy resets after every battle, so don't hold back!

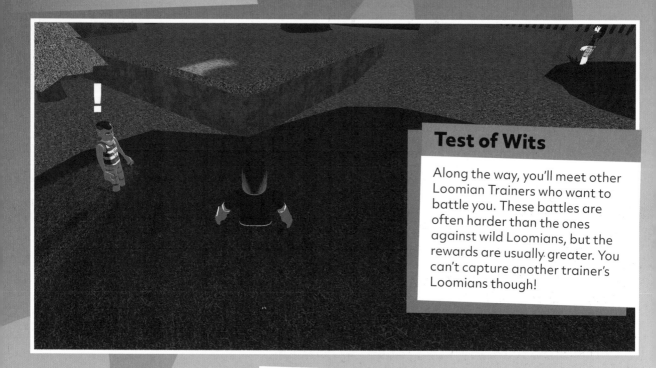

Test of Wits

Along the way, you'll meet other Loomian Trainers who want to battle you. These battles are often harder than the ones against wild Loomians, but the rewards are usually greater. You can't capture another trainer's Loomians though!

Ever-Changing Evolutions

As your Loomians battle, they'll gain experience levels, which will occasionally unlock new moves for your critter to use against enemies. If a Loomian gains enough levels, then it may evolve into a different, more powerful Loomian.

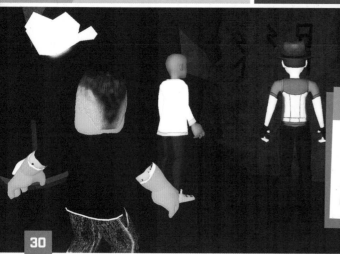

Squad Goals

You can carry up to seven Loomians at once: five that take part in battle and two that occupy the 'bench'. Benched Loomians gain a small amount of experience for every battle but can't be put in to fight.

Appy Days

The apps on your LoomiWatch can be found at the top of the screen. Using these buttons, you can sort the Loomians you want to use in battle, see each one you've met in the LoomiPedia, use items, or check out location info. It's a very handy tool!

Helping Hand

There are people across Roria that will give you hints about quests, or tasks they'd like you to complete. Talk to them to hear what they want and then return once you've completed the task. These people have yellow speech bubbles above their head.

Starring Role

As your party grows more powerful, you'll be able to visit Battle Theatres, where you can challenge great trainers called Battle Stars for the chance to win a badge. But there are a lot of other trainers standing in your way before the Battle Stars ...

THE WILD WEST

Fancy jumping on your horse and riding through the plains, hills and deserts while hunting for people, food, weapons and loot? Sure you do! The home page isn't bursting with Western titles, but The Wild West is worth checking out. It's a bit like a Jailbreak set in the 1800s with horses instead of cars and sheriffs instead of police!

CREATED BY: STARBOARD STUDIOS
YEAR: 2018
GENRE: WESTERN

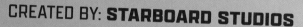

TOP TIP

Some single-action guns have the ability to fan fire, which means they have a higher firing speed but suffer with less shooting accuracy.

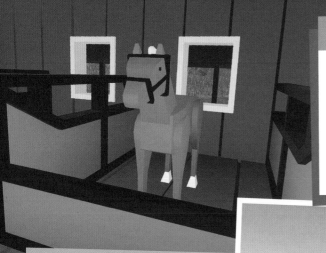

Learn Locations

Many new players opt to start in Bronze City, which is towards the centre with Copper Gulch Mine to the west and Great Plains to the south. At Bronze City, head to the stable and get yourself a horse. Players start with some cash, so see what animal you can afford. You won't get far in this game without a horse to ride!

Guns Galore

Weapons range from rifles to pistols, revolvers and shotguns, plus throwable items and melee weapons. Some basic pieces may be priced under $1000, but the best firearms will be much more expensive. Remember that weapons can also be sold if you want to get some cash back.

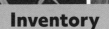

Inventory

Your inventory is kept in your backpack, which has a maximum stack of 30 items for things like weapons, tools and loot. Six backpack items can be added to your hotbar for easy access. The item you have equipped is marked with a green holstered symbol.

Night Vision

Be aware of the night! You'll be in near darkness, making your visibility poor as you move across the map in search of resources. Use the mini map at the bottom of your screen to help you move in the right direction. Call your horse to speedily get you to safe spots!

Money Maker

Taking down animals was part of the lifestyle back in the old west and you'll come across all sorts of creatures. Bears, for example, are quick, fierce and nearly always attack, but their meat sells for $50, so being brave and targeting one makes sense. Some meats are worth more when cooked first too.

Special Sheriff

Instead of robbing players, you can play as a Sheriff and keep the law in check! Two Sheriffs can operate in the same match and can get their badge by visiting the office in Bronze City. These law enforcers have a baton and handcuffs, which are unique to them and can bring outlaws to justice.

Heating Up

Meat can be cooked on a campfire purchased from a general store. They will set you back 200 bucks, but will provide a good amount of light at night. This is very helpful when you're hunting an animal or just trying to stay safe in the dark, as well as the obvious cooking bonus!

Camping Out

With wild animals roaming, you may not think camping out makes sense, but it has some benefits!
A camp bed costs $400 and restores health to anyone asleep on it. Tents have a bed inside and offer protection from animals as well as providing healing.

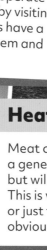

TOP TIP

For your favourite Roblox games, you can click the 'follow' icon on the main homepage and you'll be automatically notified when updates are released.

General Advice

Six general stores are dotted around the map, in spots such as Bronze City, Puerto Dorado and Howling Peak. It's the place to pick up items such as a pickaxe, axe, camping gear and other special items. The store is also the spot to sell any items you no longer want.

What's Mine Is Mine

Mining is an easier way to make money, though creatures lurk inside mines too, so keep a weapon within reach! The Copper Gulch Mine attracts plenty of people keen to collect ores, as do the Quarry, Water Cavern and Silver Hill. Use your pickaxe to start extracting ores to sell in the store. If you're lucky you'll find gems too!

Tier Time

Pickaxe tiers determine the strength of a tool – a tier 6 pick is much more powerful than a tier 2 one and will get you better ores. As soon as you can afford it, get a high-tier pickaxe and axe to get your tasks done more efficiently!

DRIVING EMPIRE

Just keep driving and racing to create your own awesome automotive empire! Everywhere you look there are cool cars, from expensive supercars to tricked-up hyper machines. But it's not just about ripping up the tarmac – you can also take to the sky or sea in helicopters and boats when you have the funds, giving you an epic all-round racing experience!

CREATED BY: WAYFORT
YEAR: 2019
GENRE: DRIVING

FUN FACT

The fastest cars in Driving Empire max out at over 300mph.

WOW!

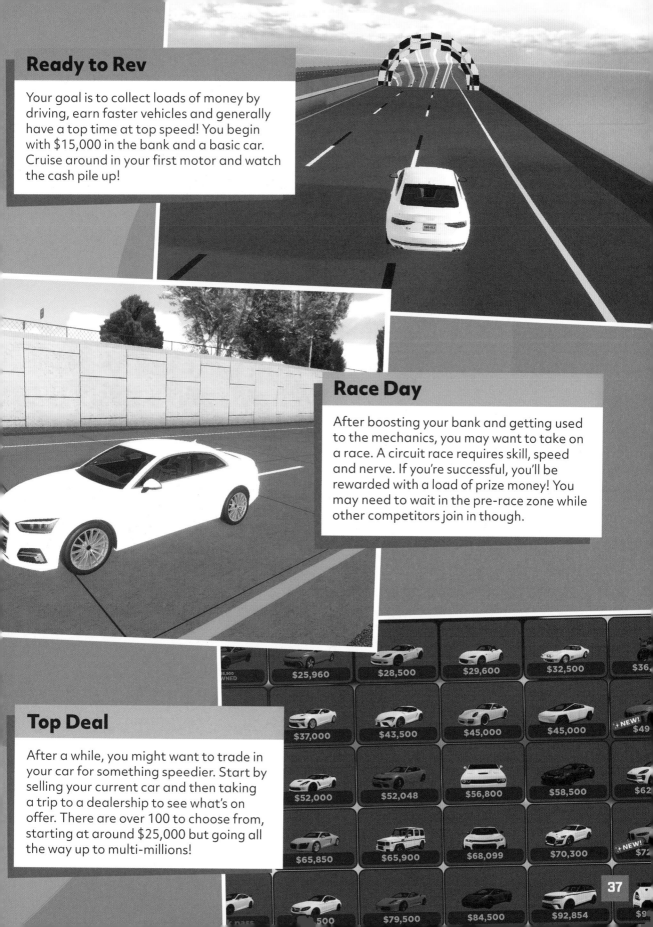

Ready to Rev

Your goal is to collect loads of money by driving, earn faster vehicles and generally have a top time at top speed! You begin with $15,000 in the bank and a basic car. Cruise around in your first motor and watch the cash pile up!

Race Day

After boosting your bank and getting used to the mechanics, you may want to take on a race. A circuit race requires skill, speed and nerve. If you're successful, you'll be rewarded with a load of prize money! You may need to wait in the pre-race zone while other competitors join in though.

Top Deal

After a while, you might want to trade in your car for something speedier. Start by selling your current car and then taking a trip to a dealership to see what's on offer. There are over 100 to choose from, starting at around $25,000 but going all the way up to multi-millions!

Teleport

If you find it difficult to navigate your way around the map, then the teleport tool comes to the rescue! Think of it as a futuristic satnav that will magic you from place to place. Select the race site you'd like to appear at, or if you're in the mood for an upgrade, instantly take yourself to a dealership.

Set Up

Take time to get your settings to your liking. The big decision is whether you want others to drive your precious cars! Choose 'nobody', 'friends' or 'everyone'. Keeping the collision setting on means a car will take damage if it hits cars or objects and you can even choose whether it plays the radio!

Reach The Limit

There's another incentive to getting better cars – going faster gives you more money! If you can regularly reach speeds of 200mph plus, your cash count rises like crazy. The Chevey and Toyoda are sensible fast cars for between $40,000 to $55,000.

Cop Cars

If you buy the police gamepass, you can take control of a classic white cop cruiser, complete with red and blue lights and able to hit speeds of over 150mph. Don't forget to pull out the police radar gun and track the speed of drivers.

Shooting Star

As well as playing police, you can choose to oppose them too! You'll get to select from a pistol or rifle, which can be used to keep the police at bay or against other bad guys. Firing accurately takes some practice but if you take down your targets, you'll look like a legend!

Bounty Hunt

A good sign of criminal success is the bounty level on your head! If a baddie has been firing their weapon, it will increase their bounty, and being caught speeding by a cop will push it even higher. If a cop arrests someone with a bounty, then they will pocket the money.

Custom Car

Get creative with the look and feel of your car. Swing by the customisation building and flick through the options you have to kit it out. Performance changes will make the biggest difference to how fast your car goes and how easy it is to handle it.

Customization

SUPER STRIKER LEAGUE

Described by the creator as extreme soccer, Super Striker gives players the power to perform extraordinary skills on the pitch and smash in some great goals! The games are quick and crazy, with small-sided teams working together to run rings around the opponents. It's kick-off time!

CREATED BY: CINDER STUDIO
YEAR: 2019
GENRE: SPORTS

TOP TIP

Reach level 25 in Super Striker League and you can trade items with other footballers.

Beginner Basics

The Beginner League eases you into the on-field action when you start, before the Novice League ups the pace. You can create a private match if you have friends playing or just join a game with randoms. Games have five players on each side (four outfield plus the keeper) and the aim is to score the most goals in four minutes!

Stadium Select

New maps and stadium scenes are added all the time. You could find yourself skidding around on the icy Polar Passage or a futuristic sports stadium. Get some games under your belt to increase your level. You need level five to access equipment and items, and level ten to start selecting new soccer abilities.

Deke Details

In this game, a 'deke' is a skill you can unleash in a match, but these must be earned as you level up. Dekes include cool abilities like a spin dash, power surge, counterattack, sidestep and basic dodge. Try them out as you unlock them to see how they can help you raise your game.

Ball Colour

No, your eyes are not playing tricks – the ball really does change colour during a match! The colour of the ball is influenced by how often it has been touched and has different effects on how it can be handled. A white ball can be hit with outrageous power and zoom into the net from distance.

Power Shot

Charge your shots and strike when you hit full power! This will give the goalkeeper little chance of saving, especially when you're at close range. You will stand still for a couple of seconds while this happens, so make sure you have the time!

Stamina

The small green bar shows your stamina level. The lower your stamina is, the more likely you are to fail actions such as passes, dodges or tackles. All these tasks take a strain on your stamina and need a few seconds to regenerate.

Kicking Cash

Striker Cash is the currency you can earn if you're winning and playing lots of games. This is what you need to buy new abilities, upgrades and items such as boots, gloves and helmets. Pro Tickets unlock rare cosmetics and booster items that give you an extra edge on the field!

FUN FACT

The trinket extraction tool lets you safely take a trinket away from any item you own so you can use it again later on.

Top Trinkets

Under the item tab you'll find a tab called trinkets. These are things like ability boosts, extra shot damage and stun reduction. Trinkets are ranked in bronze, silver and gold rarity and have a rating based on power, stamina and defence. The higher the rating, the more effective the trinket will be.

2
1
0
0

Casual Kicks

Common
462 XP (23/461)
2

⚡ 1   👟 0   🛡 0

1 Stat Points Available
Sell value: $44

Beating The Keeper

Don't be scared of the goalkeeper. You can either bend a beautiful shot from a distance or race towards the net and force the keeper out. Then make a quick spin to confuse the keeper and slot a sly shot into the corner while they are off their line.

Explosive Scenes

Throw a bomb into a match and let the chaos begin! They may be quite small and look like black footballs, but when a bomb ignites, any players caught in its blast will definitely feel it.

FUN FACT

If you collect a huge amount of points you could be crowned the Player of the Day and appear on a sign in the lobby!

Stat Attack

You'll soon become obsessed with the stats after every match. Outfield players from each team are ranked on their goals, assists, shots and passes. The Most Valuable Player (MVP) is also highlighted and is an honour that shows what a crucial team player you are.

CURSED ISLANDS

Part obstacle course, part adventure and full of frantic fun, Cursed Islands is not like any other game and is great for a laugh with friends. There's a huge slice of luck involved as you try to choose a safe island to stand on before a disaster sweeps in that could wipe you out!

CREATED BY: **SEVEN LEVELS**

YEAR: **2017**

GENRE: **NAVAL / ADVENTURE**

FUN FACT

The spaceship is one of the best shop items as you can fly around and abduct other islanders. It's out of this world!

Islands Mayhem

The game begins with 16 small islands above the water. You have a few seconds to pick one before a random event occurs. Perhaps a tornado will rip up your block? Or will giant octopus tentacles crash through and knock you out? If you're unlucky enough to be caught, then it's game over!

Survival

The pressure grows as the rounds progress. The islands reduce in numbers, giving you fewer options to seek safe haven before disasters strike. You only have a few seconds to dash around and if the rising tide catches you, you're out!

Epic Extras

You'll earn rubies and coins as you survive, which you can use to buy items in the shop. Speed and gravity boots will whizz you around and the ghostify option makes you vanish for a limited time. Cosmetic items help you stand out on the island too!

Fightback

Picking up a sword is a game changer. Use it to wipe out the other players on your island and to give you the chance to boost your rank and the EXP you earn. But beware: enemies can do the same to you!

PROJECT LAZARUS: ZOMBIES

Zombie is a word that strikes fear into most people, but in Project Lazarus you need to step up to defend civilisation. This is a total zombie shoot-up fest and you'll hardly spend more than a few seconds without having the scary creatures marching straight for you. Take them down in waves, collect rewards and upgrades in order to progress to the next relentless level.

CREATED BY: LOGITECH101
YEAR: 2016
GENRE: FIGHTING / FIRST-PERSON SHOOTER

FUN FACT

The game's creator, logitech101, based Project Lazarus: Zombies on a game they first made in 2008 called Call of Robloxia: Zombies.

Attack Time

You begin in a poorly-lit building full of random rooms, including libraries, offices and labs. Zombies will begin to break down the wooden barricades that cover the entrances and force their way through. This is your cue to launch attacks! In the early rounds, use your knife to quickly clear the gruesome invaders.

Build Barriers

Make sure you quickly repair any broken barriers and work with your teammates to keep zombies out and earn points. The points you bank can be used to buy weapons, although the first few rounds are quite easy, so there's no need to rush for expensive guns.

Head Start

One piece of weapon-wielding advice is absolutely crucial – aim for the zombie's head. This is the quickest way to wipe them out. Shots to the body do less damage, so with wave after wave coming for you, you need clean and clinical shooting!

Revive

Even experienced players can get caught out and take damage and eventually be knocked out. However, a teammate has the chance to come along and revive you, which takes about three seconds. If you are not revived, you'll exit the game and return to the lobby to start again.

Straight Lines

Zombies attack in great numbers, but thankfully they're not the smartest! They walk in a straight line and make it easy for you to nail a headshot without having to swing your aim. Often you can run past a zombie, then turn and shoot once you have more space to operate in.

Clearing Up

As well as keeping zombies barricaded, you'll need to clear debris from corridors, rooms and stairs so that you can access the rest of the building. Clearing debris will cost you points but it's a necessary spend so that you can explore further and hunt down the beasts.

Get Guns

As the difficulty increases and the intensity of waves ramps up, you'll need a weapon to match the challenge. A large collection of higher-grade machines can be bought from the walls, known as wall weapons, for between 500 to 1,500 points. These include beasts such as the AK-47 and M16.

TOP TIP

Don't get trapped in a corner by a group of zombies. Always have an escape route and space behind you to walk backwards while you tap fire.

Power Play

As you clear debris, blast zombies and enter rooms, your objective becomes clear – find the power room. Once you have gained access, flick the red switch on the wall to open up the doors on the first floor, so you can scavenge through the whole block. There should be a key to collect too.

Perk Up

Once you've visited the power room, perks are activated. They can be bought from perk machines and typically cost between 1500 and 4000 points. They can double a player's health, help them revive or fix barriers quicker and reload weapons at a faster rate. They last until you get knocked down.

Pack-A-Punch

The key from the power room is needed to open the storage room door, behind which lurks the Pack-A-Punch machine. Although it costs 5000 points to operate, it turns your guns into super shooters! The damage, fire rate, mag size and ammo capacity are all boosted, plus a special ability is added.

Zombie Drops

Power-ups are the glowing, green game-enhancing effects left behind by a zombie when you've defeated it. Drops include getting a double points ability, auto barrier rebuilds, maximum ammo and the devastating nuclear bomb. Drop a bomb and it kills every zombie currently in the level!

It's A Mystery

Dotted around the map in five locations, the mystery boxes are another way to get your hands on a high-level weapon. As the name says, the weapon inside is unknown and may or may not be an upgrade on what you currently have. It costs 950 points to open one.

Q-CLASH

Thanks to several years of development and a hardcore following, this slick-looking FPS is packed with excitement. Q-Clash is a tense team tussle, boasting game modes that call on strong defence and attacking tactics, with group objectives at the core. Deploy to the map and give the opposition nightmares!

CREATED BY: **DUCKARMOR**
YEAR: **2016**
GENRE: **FIRST-PERSON SHOOTER**

GHOST OFFENSE

TOP TIP

Q-Clash offers a reward based on consecutive days you log in and play. Keep playing and collecting the mini prizes!

Cool Clashers

There are eight 'Clashers' to choose from, although two – Cyborg and Decker P.I – begin locked and need either Robux or a heap of gems to be activated. Clashers each have a primary role – offense, defence or support. Try to balance these roles across your squad to get a good mix of abilities.

Pick a Player

For new players, Sheila and Ghost are often the easiest to take into battle. Ghost's fully automatic assault rifle has good accuracy, he also has grenades and a helpful sprint too. Sheila starts with lower health, but her dual flintlock shotguns deal deadly damage and her dive roll function gets her close to the enemy quickly.

FUN FACT

The game is incredibly well made and even has a professional voiceover cast shouting instructions and tips. Keep the audio on!

On the Attack

Unlike pretty much every other shooter you can play, the guns can't be upgraded or swapped, so make sure you pick a character you like. You can switch roles during a game and become a different Clasher though. This is a great tactic if you find your team is unbalanced or needs some firepower, for instance.

Q-CLASH

Game Mode 1

There are three core game modes to master, which are randomly selected when you enter a game. The first, Escort the Payload, calls on your team to clear a path so that your payload can follow a route through the map and safely reach its destination. Use your weapons and abilities to keep it on track.

Game Mode 2

The next mode is Capture the Hill and Defend the Hill. Look for the zoned square marked with a blue or red laser, depending on your team, then do all you can to repel enemies from reaching it. The percentage level at the top tells you how close you are to winning or losing.

Game Mode 3

Capture the Point is a similar mode, but a team's target is to take down three points on the map in a single game. Honing in on these targets requires a team to work together. If you can outnumber the enemy, your chances of wiping them out and keeping them at bay are pretty good!

Tactic Time

Shootouts in Q-Clash will often be crazy, but if you can plan ahead your success rate will increase greatly. One tactic is to squeeze enemy Clashers into tight spots, giving them little room to escape and for you to land clean hits. Finally, try to aim from high spots to down your target, because it's easier to connect and difficult for others to hit back.

Brilliant Boxes

Opening a loot box is your chance to grab cool cosmetic items of differing rarities. Some boxes are free or earned but others can be gained by using gems, the Q-Clash currency. If you're lucky, you'll get a cool skin that you can wear in your next match.

Maps

Although there are different maps, they all offer similar places to snipe, shoot and spring secret surprises from. Neo Tokyo is a busy cityscape full of high-rise blocks, indoor and outdoor settings and plenty of places to use as cover while you attack. The Castle is more open and inviting, with old buildings and grassland, but don't be fooled as the danger level is just as high as in the city.

Medals

Who doesn't love getting a shiny medal to show off? Q-Clash has loads on offer for completing in-game tasks. They may be straightforward, like playing for a certain time as a particular Clasher, or more complex, like requiring a number of eliminations with a certain weapon.

TOP TIP

Don't forget to open up and equip what's inside your free welcome loot box when you first start playing.

CREATURES OF SONARIA

Spend some time in this creature-crazy game where you battle, survive, hunt, trade and more. Creatures of Sonaria lets you choose a mythical animal and roam a fantasy island full of opportunities, adventure, challenges and ... predators! Look after your creature and work hard to help it mature, all the while keeping your eyes open for incoming danger.

CREATED BY: SONAR STUDIOS
YEAR: 2020
GENRE: SURVIVAL / ADVENTURE

TOP TIP

Not all water sources are drinkable, which means you'll need to find a new area of water so that your thirst level can rise.

Creature Creation

Don't race through your creature selection – take a few moments thinking about the type of animal you'd like and studying strengths and weaknesses. Beasts can be sorted by land, sea and sky varieties, or diet type – whether they eat plants, meat or both. Each creature has different health, appetite, damage, bleed, speed, weight and growth stats.

Early Life

You'll spawn as a baby and will need ten minutes to grow to an adult. In early life, your aims are to keep clear of predators and keep on top of your thirst, hunger and stamina levels. Hunger is boosted by eating and energy levels will quickly drop if you run or fly a lot.

Mapped Out

Your creature's surroundings have a big impact on its wellbeing. The island of Sonaria ranges from a desert oasis to rich swamps, tall forests and hot springs. Plant-eaters should avoid dunes as there's little to eat, while huge trees can block the flight path to the ground. The day cycle can also make it difficult to spot enemies in the dark too.

Awesome Abilities

The Actions function can be used all the time, whether in survival mode or in the face of attack. The options include settings such as sniffing, grazing, dragging food, dragging players and setting a nest. Sniffing will soon set a meat-eating creature onto the scent of a snack!

Calls

Actions

DINOSAUR ZOO TYCOON

Zoos are awesome fun. Dinosaurs are the most amazing creatures in history. So why not combine the two? Dinosaur Zoo Tycoon does just that and gives you a platform to build your own enclosure full of amazing prehistoric animals. If you like tycoon, role-playing and adventure games, you can spend hours creating a space to play in and impress the paying visitors.

CREATED BY: **VANITY STUDIO**
YEAR: **2021**
GENRE: **TYCOON**

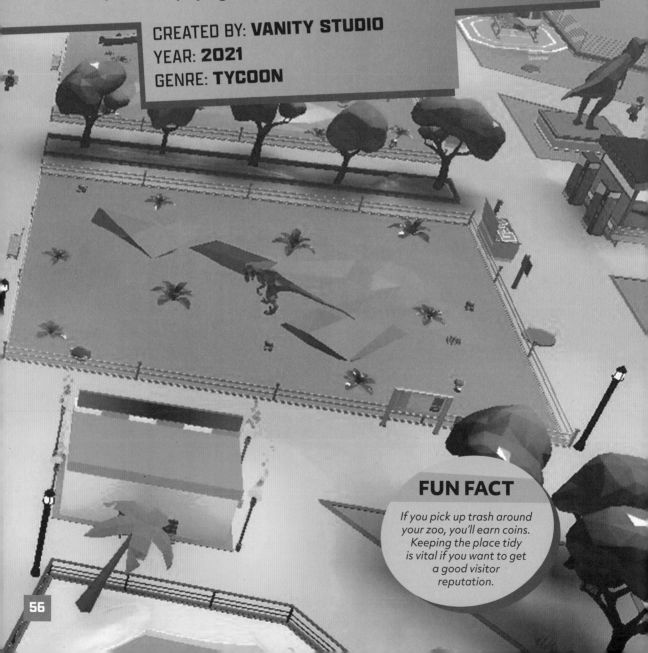

FUN FACT

If you pick up trash around your zoo, you'll earn coins. Keeping the place tidy is vital if you want to get a good visitor reputation.

Enter the Fun

Dinosaur Zoo Tycoon is really simple to set up. You're guided through opening your first zoo, from buying an entrance and ticket booth to laying a path. Keep an eye on your paycheck level. This cash is needed to add extra items, but luckily it is topped up regularly.

Dino Discovery

Benches and statues are nice, but what you really need are dinosaurs to show off. Velociraptors are the first to appear once you have made their enclosure. Watch as they are dropped in a crate from a helicopter and begin roaming around their pen! Guests will start to flock in now!

Info Stop

Read the information board by each of your enclosures to learn some cool facts. You'll discover how tall and heavy these creatures are, what they eat and all sorts of cool info. It's important to educate as well as entertain!

New Additions

Don't stop with Velociraptors – keep adding new dinos to the park once you have enough money. Oviraptors require mushrooms, plants, rocks, logs and a watering hole for their enclosure. The first of each species is free, but every additional one costs money.

DINOSAUR ZOO TYCOON

Feeding Time

Dinosaurs must be kept happy with a load of food! Some will munch on plants and others like to rip apart red meat. Just keep their bellies full with the right food, which will be placed outside their location to be picked up and given to them. The happy emoji face will show that they are well fed.

Job Hunt

Don't worry about doing ALL the work at your zoo – help is on hand! There are four jobs you can fill in the Hiring tab, using coins or Robux. The tour guide chats to people, the scientist earns you extra cash, the janitor cleans up and the dino feeder keeps the animals well fed.

Personal Touch

All the individual features you can place have a template that you must find space for, so the buildings can get a bit repetitive. You can give dinos their own name as a touch of individuality. Naming a creature after yourself is the best way to start!

Splash Out

The Splash Zone opened in 2021 and is accessed by hopping onto one of the Splash Zone buttons. You'll be transported to an aquatic arena, where the attention switches from land-based dinos to those that thrive in water. Huge see-through water tanks appear and become home to weird wonders such as the aquatic dunkleosteus and gigantic elasmosaurus. Awesome!

Fossil Finds

As well as bringing dinosaurs back to life and showing them off, you can also search for fossils. Just follow the instructions and dig in the proper areas, collecting fragments and items to identify later. At this zoo, you need to keep your eyes peeled for what's above and below the ground!

Cool Stuff

Build the arctic zone in Dinosaur Zoo Tycoon and scary dudes like bison, mammoths and saber-toothed tigers will add a cool new attraction for the guests. Create their enclosures in the same way you have for the raptors, T-rex and others, but just remember to chuck in plenty of snow!

Fun Stuff

You can also add theme park attractions to really put a smile on visitors' faces. After you have played for a while, you have the option to place a ferris wheel and carousel. Along with the balloon stand, ice cream stalls and gift shop, there's always plenty to do!

TOP TIP

When your zoo gets bigger, just use the teleport tool to quickly zap you from place to place in no time.

SEE YA NEXT TIME!

What a ride through Robloxia you've been on! The games you've discovered in this great guide have taken you from dangerous and mysterious islands to city shootouts, fantastical quests, futuristic football fields, crazy zoos and beyond. It's just a glimpse of what Roblox offers to the millions of gamers who load it up and enjoy the adventures in front of them.

As you've seen, the action is endless. The Roblox homepage constantly updates with new stuff and there's always a reason to jump in. Search for team-based combat games, role-playing simulators, tycoon tests or a frantically fun experience for you and your friends. If you find an awesome new game, tell your mates
and share the strategies and secrets you'll need to master it!

All the games are made by people just like you; Roblox fans who want to offer a cool time for the rest of the community. There's nothing to stop you building your own game in the future through the Roblox Studio too.

Keep playing and keep enjoying the fun scenes on your screen.

Laters, gamers!

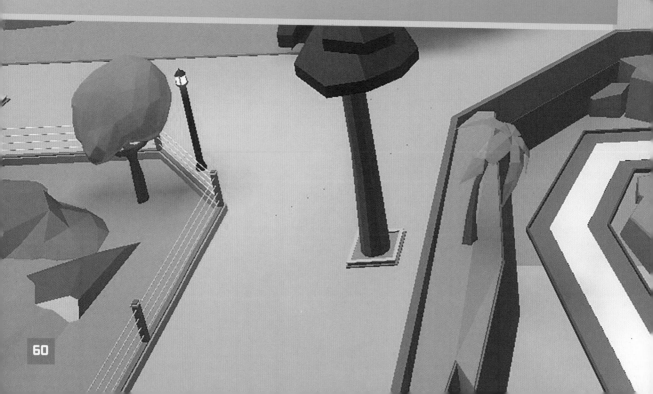

YOUNGER FANS' GUIDE TO ROBLOX

Roblox might be your first experience of digital socializing, so here are a few simple rules to help you stay safe and keep the internet a great place to spend time.

■ Never give out your real name – don't use it as your username.

■ Never give out any of your personal details.

■ Never tell anybody which school you go to or how old you are.

■ Never tell anybody your password except a parent or guardian.

■ Always tell a parent or guardian if something is worrying you.

Stay safe online. Any website addresses listed in this book are correct at the time of going to print. However, Farshore is not responsible for content hosted by third parties. Please be aware that online content can be subject to change and websites can contain content that is unsuitable for children.
We advise that all children are supervised when using the internet.

PARENTS' GUIDE TO ROBLOX

Roblox has security and privacy settings that enable you to monitor and limit your child's access to the social features on Roblox, or turn them off completely. You can also limit the range of games your child can access, view their activity histories and report inappropriate activity on the site.

To restrict your child from playing, chatting and messaging with others on Roblox, log in to your child's account and click on the gear icon in the upper right-hand corner and select Settings. From here you can access the Security and Privacy menus:

- Users register for Roblox with their date of birth. It's important for children to enter the correct date because Roblox has default security and privacy settings that vary based on a player's age – this can be checked and changed in Settings.

- To review and restrict your child's social settings go to Settings and select Privacy. Review the options under Contact Settings and Other Settings. Select No one or Everyone. Note: players age 13 and older have additional options.

- To control the safety features that are implemented on your child's account, you'll need to set up a 4-digit PIN. This will lock all of the settings, only enabling changes once the PIN is entered. To enable an Account PIN, go to the Settings page, select Security and turn Account PIN to ON.

To help monitor your child's account, you can view the history for certain activities:

- To view your child's private message history, choose Messages from the menu bar down the left-hand side of the main screen. If the menu bar isn't visible, click on the list icon in the left-hand corner.

- To view your child's chat history, open the Chat & Party window, located bottom-right. You can then click on any of the listed users to open a window with the chat history.

- To view your child's online friends and followers, choose Friends from the menu bar down the left-hand side of the main screen.

- To view your child's creations, choose Develop from the tabs running along the top of the main screen.

- To view any virtual items purchased and any trade history, choose Trade from the menu bar then go to My Transactions.

While the imagery on Roblox has a largely blocky, digitized look, parents should be aware that some of the user-generated games may include themes or imagery that may be too intense for young or sensitive players:

- You can limit your child's account to display only a restricted list of available games to play. Go to Settings, select Security and turn on Account Restrictions.

Roblox players of all ages have their posts and chats filtered to prevent personal information being shared, but no filter is foolproof. Roblox asks users and parents to report any inappropriate activity. Check your child's account and look to see if they have friends they do not know. Talk to your child about what to report (including bullying, inappropriate behavior or messages, scams and other game violations):

- To report concerning behavior on Roblox, use the Report Abuse links located on game, group and user pages and in the Report tab of every game menu.

- To block another player during a game session, find the user on the leaderboard/player list at the upper-right of the game screen. (If the leaderboard/player list isn't there, open it by clicking on your username in the upper-right corner.) From here, click on the player and select Block User.

For further information, Roblox has created a parents' guide to the website, which can be accessed at https://corp.roblox.com/parents